Notes From the Teacher's Desk

Angela Fang

Notes From the Teacher's Desk © 2023
Angela Fang

All rights reserved.

No part of this publication may be reproduced, stored in a retrieval system, or transmitted, in any form or by any means, electronic, mechanical, photocopying, recording, or otherwise, without the prior written permission of the presenters.

Angela Fang asserts the moral right to be identified as the author of this work.

Presentation by *BookLeaf Publishing*

Web: www.bookleafpub.com

E-mail: info@bookleafpub.com

ISBN: 9789358367768

First edition 2023

*I dedicate this book to Cameron Dyer; thank
you for pushing me to actually stop telling the
stories and start writing them! Without you,
this would not have happened!*

*Also, to all my beautiful daughters, Cozette,
Sagan, Faith, Emma and Azure, I know having
a teacher for a mom could not have been easy!
I love you all to the moon and back!*

ACKNOWLEDGEMENT

I acknowledge all the amazing students, teachers, and principals that have encouraged and even hampered me along the way! Without them, I wouldn't be the teacher I am today!

PREFACE

Ms. Fang has been chained to this desk for over twenty-three years. Today she walks away. She's taught over 500 scholars everything from tying their shoes, blowing their nose, to staying quiet and don't move if there's an intruder on the school grounds. She's ending her teaching career with a smile and a heart full of the endearing tales that she's sharing here as "Notes from the teacher's desk."

Do I Really Want to Do This?

Dear Ms. Fang,
Teaching was not my first choice.
I wanted to work with children.
I knew what children needed,
having grown up in poverty, and abuse.
I wanted to HELP children.
But, not teach, everyone in Oklahoma teaches.
If you are a girl and you go to college you
either get a M.R.S. degree or a teaching degree.
I have to decide on what I want to do.
Psychology, let's try that.
No way, all that brain science, I'm not smart
enough for that.
Come on, Angela, What are you going to do?
Social Work? Yes, let's do that!
No, too much government bureaucracy,
I can't really help the kids.
So, back to teaching. I can't stay in college
forever.
As it is, it's going to take me two more years.
How long did it take for you to become a
teacher?
Six YEARS, six long years.
I could have become a doctor.
But, teaching? Really?

I guess I'll try it.
Good Luck,
Ms. Fang

Getting the Job.

Dear Ms. Fang,
I did it! I really did it!
First, and only one out of my ten siblings
that went to college, and actually graduated!
I did this thing!
I passed all the classes, did all the projects,
then passed all the certifications!
I did it!

Now, onto the actual teaching.
Where do I get a job? How do I get a job?
Job fair at my college?
I think I'll go!

So many principals, superintendents,
future teachers all mingling through

the building. They are spitting words at me,
acronyms really, not words.
IEP, Title1, EOY, BOY, MOY, test scores.
What is this language?

Lake Worth, ISD. Title 1 school!
Wow, that's impressive, TITLE1!
They must have won first place to be a Title1
School!
Sure I'll come there! I'd love to teach for you!
Starting Salary, $26,000! YES!!
That's the money train!

"Texas, that's awesome! That's
where the money is at!" Everyone told me.
I didn't really care about money, I wanted to help
the kids.
But, eating would be nice too!

So, we loaded the U-haul, and
away we went, to this beautiful
TITLE 1 School!
Moving On,
Ms. Fang

Anticipation...

Dear Ms. Fang,
Exciting...That's what this is!
We have moved!
We packed it all up, and headed to Texas!
This is going to be so great!
A state I've never lived in.
We will know no one!
All on our own!

Terrifying...That's what this is!
We literally know no one,
I can't drive here,
where is my new school?
How many lanes of traffic are there?

Nervous...That's what I am!
I've decorated, scrubbed, painted.
I've sewn pillows, made name tags
for all 27 of my new kindergartners!
I've got two that are going to be severely
mentally disabled, I got this!
I have no problem dealing
with children who have disabilities.
Give me all the hard cases too!

Nervous, they are coming tomorrow!
Shaking in my shoes,
Ms. Fang

New to This.

Dear Ms. Fang,
I'm here bright and early!
So eager to see all my sweet kiddos faces.
They will be pouring through that door in ten
minutes!
I'm so excited, and nervous, and what if they
don't like me?
I want them all to LOVE me!

They are here. I greet them at the door.
They cling to their parents. I forgot this is new to
them too!
I show them their spots, their cubbies,
where to hang their backpacks,
and my sweet little yellow clawfoot bathtub

painted with my niece's handprints, with
hand-sewn pillows
overflowing the space.
It's my reading center!
They can climb inside and quietly read books to
themselves or each other.

Oh God, Johnny is crying. He won't let go of
mom's hand.
Do I pull him away? Tell mom to go?
No one told me they wouldn't want to be here
with me!
Why wouldn't they tell me?
I feel the panic rising up in my chest.
I may vomit!
What do I do?

Ok, eye-level, tell him how scared you are.
Make a connection,
Wait he's taking my hand,
he's walking away with me!
Wave goodbye to mom!
He's smiling at me!
I can do this!
Now let's do breakfast,
Ms. Fang

Ms. Fang, you're anointing!

Dear Ms. Fang,
Teaching is hard.
How do I keep up with all of the paperwork?
I'm teaching kindergarten!
How many forms do I need to complete?
They are five years old!
How do I keep it all straight?

Justin is hard.
How do I teach him?
He's defiant, and emotionally disturbed.
How do I reach him?
His mom is not supportive.
How do I get them to like me?
"Ms. Fang, my mom says you're anointing."

How do I tell him, "I'm sure she means
annoying!"?

There's 27 of these five-year-olds.
How do I make them read?
There's 27 little, squirmy children.
How do I make them understand addition,
subtraction?
There's 27 beautiful, amazing babies.
How do I get them to know I love them?

I guess it's time to show them!
Love,
Ms. Fang

Title One..

Dear Ms. Fang,

Title One, by the way is the majority of your
students are below the poverty level.
Contrary to what I believed, on year one, it isn't
a prestigious award. We didn't win first place,
we weren't recognized as being the school of the
year. There were no trophies for us. No parades,
no prizes.

What we did have was homelessness,
absenteeism, malnutrition, mental abuse,
physical abuse, dirty clothes, no pencils for
homework, no food at home, and sometimes, no
parents at home. We had parents that worked
two and three jobs, there wasn't time for reading
with their child, there wasn't time or money for
projects, or fun field trips. No new clothes, or
Christmas presents.

What we had in our classroom was family. Did
we get on each other's nerves? Did we "anoint"
each other? Absolutely. However, we were a
team! We cheered for each other, cried for each
other, and absolutely loved each other. Even

though the students may have not learned all
their letter sounds, those kids knew I loved
them, the parents knew I cared for their children.

We cried and hugged that last day of school.
They gave me a plaque that appropriately said,
"We love you, our first teacher! Love your first
kingergarten class." Yes, it's spelled wrong, but
it's somehow appropriate for that first year. We
spelled plenty of stuff wrong, but we loved,
"KINGERGARTEN"!

Love,
Ms. Fang

You don't want me?

Dear Ms. Fang,
March!
I've almost done it, almost!
I've fulfilled all of my duties, almost!
I've passed all of my Texas Certifications,
almost!

April!
It's time for my final evaluation!
It's time for the principal to come see my
teaching skills!
It's time for my students to shine!

May!
We aren't asking you back for the next school
year...

We don't think you met our expectations...
We are going in a different direction...

June!
What do I do with this degree?
What did I do wrong?
What am I going to do if I can't teach?

July!
Why wasn't I what they wanted?
Why can't I be a teacher at that school?
Why don't they want me?

August!
Send out one more application,
Call one more principal,
Go to yet another interview,
Wait, what exactly is this?
Private School?

OK, Let's try that!
Something New,
Ms. Fang

See you at C.U!

Ms. Fang,
This place is a fairy tale!
There's a yellow brick road, and a castle.
The teachers dress in costume for all the events!
And, there are events!

This is definitely not Title One!
Private school, I went from below poverty level
to parents telling me they signed my paycheck.
They aren't technically wrong!

There's smiles, and giggles.
Exciting new adventures to be done!
Parents parade in with their pretty princesses and
little kings
all clean and shiny.

The nerves are back.
I don't know how to do rich people.
I grew up Title One, how do I deal with the
entitled?

Smile, and straighten my skirt.
Rich or poor, they are still kids.
They are still five year olds.
They still run, skin their knees,
and I still fix everything with a bandaid.

Sing the ABCs, rock around the clock,
and add the apples. The basics stay the same.
This is a different world though.
I remind myself, I went to college for this.
I'm the expert, even when the adults make me
feel like dirt.

It will get better, right?
Hopefully,
Ms. Fang

CU, It's the Place to Be!

Ms. Fang!
You will never guess what they have here!
Goats, chickens, pigs, and even a llama!
This place is a dream.
Too good to be true, it may seem!

I keep waiting for the other shoe to fall,
I went from my students not having food to eat,
to this school having a garden where food rots
on the vine.
The learning experiences these children have is
top-tier.
There's a major difference in Title 1 and private
school.

This school is a place I can stay.

It's where I would want my kids to go.
They are reading by four years old.
I imagine becoming tenured here.
Never having to find another school!

CU, is the place to be!
Ms. Fang

A RED Pen!

Dear Ms. Fang,
How dare you embarrass a student like that?
You graded a spelling test with a RED pen!
He may never have the confidence to be
somebody, someday!

A RED pen, circled the eighteen out of twenty
spelling words he missed.
Sigh...
My job now hangs in the balance because I
chose to use a RED pen.

I crumple into my chair.
I can't catch my breath.
How dare I use a RED pen?

How about the fact that your child didn't study
for the test?
Or, that he didn't even try?
Now, we will have a meeting over my RED
pen...

The father yells at me, "How dare you?"
He tells me, "You are so stupid!"

"Do you know what you have done to my child's
self-esteem?" He asks.
He screams at me, "I sign your paycheck!"

"It's just a RED pen," I stammer.
"One she will never use again," Agrees the
director.
Matter discussed, case closed.
She's right, from now on I'll use MAGENTA!

With a RED Flair,
Ms. Fang

Tour of Texas

Ms. Fang,
This school has such amazing opportunities!
It is definitely the place to be!
There is lots of joy and learning.

This year I moved up to teach 4th grade.
4th grade? What was I thinking?
I don't even know where to begin.

First, I must plan the field trip.
The field trip of a lifetime, in 4th grade,
my students will spend five days caravanning
across Texas!

Each child, has to have their parents with them.
So, now I'm in charge of 25 students, and their
parents.
How do I do this? How do I even start?

Museums, bat cruises, so many reservations to
make.
So much money to collect, each family has
activities to pay for.
Movies, the Alamo, Waco, Dr. Pepper.

It's going to be so much fun...and so very, very
exhausting.

Take a deep breath and start making the calls.
Pay the deposits, make the reservations.
It's going to be a blast!

The eyes of Texas are upon us!
Deep in the heart of Texas,
Ms. Fang

What the??? A Goat what??

Dear Ms. Fang,
Today I start my 12th year at CU.
It's my 13th year as a teacher.
This school is definitely an interesting place to
be.

However, today I was told we are hosting a
wedding!
A beautiful, day to be planned by our
sixth-grade
wedding planning, elective. Because who
doesn't plan
weddings in sixth grade?

This wedding is for who?
It's for what?
Goats? Our goats are getting married!?

We are spending how much money on this?
Every student, in every grade level has to dress
formally.
There will be a cake, a feast, and even a limo to
drive us around the block.

I just can't get over the fact that it is for, goats...
Baaaa, baaaa, baaaa,
Ms. Fang

Court

Dear Ms. Fang,
Today, my appearance has been requested
to testify for the father of one of my students.
I have taught this little girl three different times.

She was in one of my summer pre-kindergarten
classes.
I was then her teacher in 3rd grade, and when I
moved to 4th
it was her class I looped up with. I have taught
this little girl
for at least four years.

Every student becomes one of my children every
year.
No matter, how many students I have or how
many years it has been.

Once, you are one of my students, you are now one of my children.

Each year I had this little girl, she surprised me by how big her heart was!
She was the first to encourage others, she cheered everyone on, and now that she's an adult, she still does! I often get little encouraging emails, texts, or Facebook tags that remind me of why I do what I do!

Today, was going to be a hard day. Court is unfortunately a very real side of my job. Divorce and custody are something they don't prepare teachers for. They don't tell you in your Children's Literature class that one day you are going to have to sit on the witness stand, be sworn in, and testify who has been the better parent for your student. Your educational law class doesn't even prepare you for having to track whether your students have eaten that day, as you might be called on to report that in court.

I sat there and honestly reported and fortunately it worked out. It doesn't always happen that way. She was allowed to stay with her father, and stay in our school! I have had the honor and privilege to watch her grow up into a brilliant, beautiful, caring young lady! I was invited to her high school graduation, and I surprised her by being there.

I needed her, and she needed me. She reminded me why I am a teacher. So often we get wrapped up in the daily stuff and forget to look at the life stuff. She helps me remember! She likes to say I changed her life, but she will probably never really understand how she changed mine!
Love,
Ms. Fang

Death comes in the Night

Dear Ms. Fang,
A former student died today.
I don't know how to process that.
He thought he had heartburn,
because he swallowed his gum.
He went to sleep and never woke up.
His heart just stopped working.

I'm not supposed to outlive my students.
This feeling of sadness is so hard to express.
I fully love each and every one of my students,
I still use my Texas phone number almost
ten years later, just in case one of my former
students may need to contact me.

I have a snow globe this student gave me in
2001.

He was a kindergartner in my class.
He laughed and danced all the time!
This child was an absolute delight.

I put this snow globe out every year on my shelf
of treasures
I've collected from my students.
I remember when he gave it to me.
His family had just returned from Disney World.
He had carried that snow globe all over the park
because
he knew I would love it.
His mom had tried to talk him into getting me
something smaller,
something less fragile. He refused because he
just knew I would need it.

Little did we know how fragile he was.
I do need that snow globe.
Every year I take it out of its summer storage
box,
I wipe it down and look at his name scrawled
across the bottom.
I play the music, and remember him dancing and
smiling.

I miss that smile.
Sadly,
Ms. Fang

A Horse of Course...

Ms. Fang,

I teach in the hood. Middle of Gang Central in Oklahoma City! Believe it or not, we aren't still cowboys and tepees. We have a very high crime rate, and my students come from these streets. Our school has a very tiny playground, which my 5th graders have mostly outgrown. We are very fortunate though that we are located right down the street, two blocks away from a giant park the children love going to. It's big enough for the kids to spread out, play basketball, soccer, swing, slide or just sit and gossip about all the cute boys!

However, we as teachers, have to be extra vigilant the entire time we are at the park. The random things the children come across are enough to keep us on our toes. I had one student come up to me last week carrying a long stick, stuck through the bottom of the stick, I thought she was waving a deflated balloon. Do you see where this is going? It wasn't a balloon, but rather a used condom. She's parading around with it attached to the end of a stick! I made her throw the stick and all into the trash and sanitize her hands repeatedly!

We have had to abandon the park on several occasions as news helicopters start circling over. Usually circling over a drug deal gone wrong, or the year a truck deliberately drove through a front yard and hit my student's father, cutting his leg off at the hip. We as teachers quickly learn that when the helicopters show up we line up and quickly return to school.

We never know what to expect. One year, a standoff was going on across the street, with our school put on lockdown. There was a rough minute when we realized we were also on lock down…outside on the way back from the park. They had locked down the school and locked us outside!

Today, we traveled down to the park. We were enjoying the spring breezes, the students were

breaking off into their groups of soccer players, football players, and gossipers. The helicopters started circling, we rounded up the students and began to rush them back to school. A man came racing across the park right under the trees where we had just been standing. We were a little disconcerted about what he was running from or why he was running in our direction! Then through the low-hanging branches racing right towards us was the cutest miniature black pony! We all just burst out laughing! We were anticipating a gun-toting gang banger, or a police officer chasing a criminal. Not today, just a tiny little miniature pony reaching back to its passion of being the mustang and running free! Run Free Little Pony! Run Free!
Ms. Fang

Don't Mess With the Ticonderoga Pencil!

Happy Halloween Ms. Fang,
I thought you'd enjoy a scary story for a change! All teachers love a Ticonderoga pencil. It is the best writing tool! It is also the only one I allow in my classroom. Today's tale is brought to you, just for your reading pleasure! Enjoy!

I smiled slowly as I watched the blood blossom out across her white shirt. The yellow number 2 pencil wobbled gently side to side as she gasped slowly for each labored breath. It jutted out of the side of her throat and the blood continued to drip down her chest. She whispered, "Why?"

I wish I could tell her why. But, as we all know, pencils can't talk. At least they don't normally talk to people.

When did I start hearing the small voice of that writing apparatus? Was it when I picked it up in the hallway? I had rescued it from the janitor's trash. She had swept it all into a pile to be brushed into the dustpan to never be seen again. I saw the bright yellow flash, and me being the industrious teacher I am, I knew that Ticonderoga pencil did not belong with the spit wads, used Kleenex, & candy wrappers.

It seemed to gleam with happiness at its rescue. Odd, I know, it's a freaking pencil! I tucked it quickly behind my ear. Ticonderoga pencils are like gold to teachers. We secretly steal them from each others' desks, "borrow" them from students, and rescue them from all desperate situations. You'd be surprised what a teacher would go through to have Ticonderoga pencils for their classroom.

The pencil comfortably rested behind my earlobe. I went about my day, and didn't think anything else of it. My neighbor teacher, Ms. Brown, from across the hall came over to share another story of how horrible her students were for the day. I could feel the annoyance of her presence rise. I reached up and grabbed the pencil and absentmindedly began scratching my head with the eraser. Quiet whispers began to emanate my thoughts. "Just stab her in the throat. She'll stop talking!" I heard it again, and the third time I heard it, I flung the pencil across the room.

"Did you hear that?" I gasped.

"I didn't hear anything," Ms. Brown whispered. Ms. Brown stared in shock. She looked at me, and said, "I'll come back later." She quickly turned around and left the classroom.

I walked across the room, picked up the pencil, placed it behind my ear and shook my head in disbelief. Pencils don't talk I thought to myself. Ms. Brown walked back in and I heard the door swing closed behind her. "I almost forgot to tell you…" She drew in a sharp breath as I jabbed the pencil into the soft part of her throat right below her ear.

I sat down and continued grading papers.

"Maybe now she will finally be quiet," I thought to myself. Wait, I stood back up, grabbed the pencil, used her white shirt to wipe off the blood. I tucked the pencil carefully behind my ear. Ms. Brown slumped slowly to the floor.

This is purely make-believe, we all know I'd never abuse a Ticonderoga that way!

Hahaha,

Ms. Fang

This is Not a Drill.

Ms. Fang,

"Lockdown! Take lockdown procedures Now!"
My youngest daughter, Emma, another teacher
and I all looked at each other as we stopped our
copy machines. This is not how any teacher
wants to start their day. We scanned the copy
room for every viable entrance and exit. Neither
of the two doors actually closed all the way, or
even came close to locking. That's when my cell
phone began to ring. My eleven-year-old called
because she was upstairs in my classroom with
no way to lock down.

She says, "Momma, what do I do?" Her
voice shook as I tried to whisper the instructions
on how to get my classroom keys out of my bag,
how to turn the key all the way to the left to lock
it, then slightly right, and jiggle them just a little
bit to physically lock the door. She, being more

calm than I, asked if she could just run to another teacher's classroom?

"Yes! Yes! Please do that!" The relief I felt as the other teacher embraced her and locked her in her classroom I cannot physically put into words. One of my daughters was sort of safe! Now what to do to keep the one trembling beside me worried about her sister's safety. What the hell was going on? It was 7:45 a.m. the doors to the school had not even opened. Who could be threatening our elementary school already this morning?

We turned off the lights, closed both doors and tried to hide behind a shelf of books. That's when the reality of the situation hit us. We had no idea what the threat was, but what we did know was we were in a room with two unlocked doors, three metal shelves of books, and that was all that was protecting us from whatever was out there. We glanced at both doors nervously. If someone comes through one of those doors what could we possibly do? We decide to move to the farthest row of bookshelves. We army crawled along the floor, fear mounting at every sound out in the hallway. The building had an eerie silence, which intensified the creaks and groans of the building as the noises echoed down the empty hallways. My youngest daughter took deep breaths trying not to let the panic overtake her. I squeezed her hand and tried to mouth words of encouragement to her. But, how do I encourage her? I'm the mother, I'm supposed to be the hero protecting her from danger. However, I had no idea what the threat was, or where it was coming from. Was it actually coming from inside the building? Where were our eight hundred students that should be entering the building?

Intercom click, "Yes, we are coming out of lockdown, it had to be a misunderstanding!" This was the thought that entered my mind. The quaver in my principal's voice as she reiterated that, "WE ARE IN LOCK DOWN! Lock your doors, pull any scholars into the rooms with you!", spoke volumes more than her actual words.

Emma, my baby girl squeezed my hand harder and took a raggedy breath and choked back the fear rising up. The helpless feeling that raced up from the pit of my stomach caused my breakfast to lurch and the tears to form at the corners of my eyes. I just told myself I couldn't start crying! I had to hold them back, keep it together. What if the intruder heard me struggling to keep it together?

Guys, I'm a second-grade teacher! I went to college for six years to become a teacher. I wanted to help children. I wanted to teach them ABCs, how to read, to write, even how to add and subtract. This is what I signed up for. Now, there was a very real threat and even though there weren't students with me at this very moment I began questioning what exactly I had signed up for! I promise you this was not it! Don't misunderstand me here, I will die protecting your child if they are in my classroom, but I did not, in any way, sign up for crouching in a corner waiting for whatever threat was on the other side of the doorway.

Emma squeezed my hand again. I could physically feel her fear mounting. What was going on? Finally, the intercom clicked again to tell us we had switched to secure lockout and we could breathe again. Are you asking yourself what put us there? How did a school of over 800+ people just stop functioning and run to hide in corners like frightened mice?

At 7:45 a.m., an older student is banging on the outside door of our school trying to get into the building. A teacher coming into the building told the student to move away from the door. The young man turned to her and pulled a weapon from his pants. This is when the teacher realized this young man was not one of our elementary students. She immediately placed herself between the throng of students lining up to come inside to have a warm breakfast, and this weapon-wielding maniac. There are varying accounts to what the weapon actually was. Some say they saw him reach and take out a gun, others say a machete. Either way it was a weapon and he had it waving it at our students. This teacher was the only thing standing in his way, as he yelled, "GIVE ME THE KIDS!" This teacher immediately put herself in harm's way for our scholars, and the safety of all of us on the other side of those glass doors. She called our principal and the police. We locked down. He ran off. This day began what is now two months of weekly lockdowns and a terror storm so frustrating I have students that will cry when they hear the intercom click on and off.

After all of that, the bell rang, our students came in, we had another day of teaching and learning. We spoke softer to our students, hugged them tighter, and loved each other a little more. When did this become the new normal?
Still Shaking,
Ms. Fang

The Hoodie

Ms. Fang,

Today I sewed a hoodie. A dirty, smelly,
worn-out Punisher hoodie. It took me
about five minutes. As I was sewing this hoodie,
a mildly funny thought came to my head. "I
went to college for this?" I wasn't upset I was
sewing the hoodie. I was thinking about how this
small act of sewing for five minutes was going
to change Gabe's whole day. Maybe his whole
week.

I am a teacher. I teach 5th graders in a failing
school, in SOUTHSIDE Oklahoma. If
you are from that area you understand the
emphasis put on the SOUTHSIDE in that
statement. A predominantly Hispanic
neighborhood where the kids scream and laugh

at the park during the afternoon, and gunshots,
drug deals, and the Southside Vato Locos of the
Mexican Mafia rule the nights.
At least once a month, our school is on lock-out
because the police are looking for
someone in the neighborhood. As teachers we
have to stay hyper-vigilant that our outside
school doors are locked so one of these bad guys
don't get inside and decide to use our students
for leverage in a hostage situation.
Some days it is a war zone outside the school,
and sometimes the war zone is inside the school,
inside my classroom, and even in my head.

Today, as I sat sewing I reflected how if this was
my personal child's hoodie I would have just
thrown it away. The tear was long and right
where the front pouch is. The stitching won't
hold up long, but it is getting to be spring and
maybe he won't need it to last much longer. It
didn't seem to be worth saving. However, I
knew this was this child's only jacket and the
early morning air was still pretty chilly. This
jacket also symbolized something much more
profound to this child. It was his sense of
security. The one thing he owned, the one thing
that was simply HIS. Our students get passed
around a lot. This family member is raising him,
or that family member. Dad or Mom is in and

out of jail. He's in DHS custody, or with a foster
parent. He might be the oldest of 12 born to a
meth-addicted mom, who's had more than one
brush with death and the law. When you are one
of twelve, you very rarely get something new. It
is usually passed down multiple times, picked up
at a garage sale, or gotten from a Good Will
store.

This jacket had been new when Gabe received
it! It hadn't been his brother's, his
cousin's or from the Good Will this time! This
jacket was something he had worked for. He had
mowed his neighbor's yard for a month to pay
for it. He had to wait an extra two months for the
money because his mom had borrowed it to pay
the water bill. I remembered how proud he had
been when he walked into class. Hood pulled
down low over his eyes. I let him keep it like
that for an extra couple of minutes before I
reminded him about the school's policy with
hooded jackets.

That was September. It was still too warm for a
hooded jacket, but not for the
students at my school. They wear their hoodie
every day of the year. I've had students come up
to me sweating buckets on the playground.
Gasping for breath, "Ms. Fang, it's so hot out

here!" I suggest they come out of their jackets and they look at me like I've asked them to slap a puppy. These hoodies are my kids' safety blankets. They wrap themselves inside them and actually live in them. Some sleep in them, they don't have blankets, or for that fact, some don't have beds.

I've watched Gabe's jacket become faded, the decal on the front start peeling off,
and now in March it has torn. I saw it happen. He put his hands in the pocket in the front, protectively pulling it down around the rest of his body. Then it just tore. It ripped right from the pocket down. I saw the terror on his face and knew I had to do everything I could to save this possession for him.
The delight I saw in his face when I gave the hoodie back to him was worth the
skipping of my lunch. My cold, ham sandwich would wait. Giving Gabe his security, confidence, and safety back wouldn't.
I do love my students!
Love,
Ms. Fang

Is that you, Ms. Fang?

Ms. Fang,
"Teacher Tired," is a real thing.
We make every decision little or big
for however many little people are in our
classrooms.
I literally decide if this person really has to go to
the bathroom
or are they just bored and want to play around in
the hallways!
I do that for 23 little bodies a day, and since I'm
also the team lead,
Sometimes, I do that for five or more adults a
day!

My brain is mush! Every night when I go home,

I tell my husband I will make dinner, I just need
to know what to make.
I can't make any more decisions for the day!
I'm done!

This, "teacher tired," carries over into our
day-to-day life.
We start the school year in heels, dresses, and
makeup.
We end the year in sweats, coffee-stained
t-shirts, messy buns
and no makeup.

Hopefully we have washed our faces, and
brushed our teeth.
But, honestly I am not going to promise that!
However, last week I pulled it together because I
had an
interview after school.

I curled my hair, put on my makeup, my new
interview clothes, even remembered my
earrings!
Feeling rejuvenated, after three cups of coffee,
I sat at my table.

One of my sweet little people,
came up to my table. He got really close to my
face.

He made eye contact the whole time.
He stepped back about three feet,
with a trembling voice, he asked,
"Ms. Fang, is that you?"

Now, I realize teacher tired, might translate to
dead man walking...
Need a nap,
Ms. Fang

Goodbyes...

Dear Ms. Fang,
Goodbyes are hard.
During the school year,
you learn to love every child in your classroom.

You smile when they say hello in the morning.
You help bandage them up when they skin their
knee.
They bring you creepy crawly things that you
investigate together.
They also bring you squished weeds they've
picked for you.

After 23 years of teaching, the goodbyes don't
get easier.
I still cry at the end of May when they will pack
up their broken crayons,
chewed up pencils, and moldy fruit that has been
smashed in the back of their desks.

I cry when they wave their final goodbyes as
they run out of my classroom.
I cry harder when they run back in for one last
hug!
Goodbyes are hard.

I'm not crying, you're crying!
Love,
Ms. Fang